Advance Praise for
Pulse and Weave

In part an homage to the natural world, Liz Nakazawa's first full-length poetry collection reveals its author as more than a keen observer of birds, clouds, trees, flowers, and bodies of water. Turning to the human heart, she suggests that it's our job to "hold others steady." Visiting a Japanese Garden in bad weather, the poet disciplines herself: "I imagine instead of fog / a sunny day / and then decide / no, I promise to love this brash rain." And immediately she turns to watch a koi as it "swims through branches" of a dogwood reflected in a pond. Nakazawa's poems are inhabited by the spirit of the best haiku in their sparse diction and exacting thought, the poet someone "no longer busking for love" but *in love* with the plenitudinous offerings of the world and with the way "benevolent negation / strengthens what remains."

—Andrea Hollander, Author of *Blue Mistaken for Sky*

Liz Nakazawa's *Pulse and Weave* brings us poems emanating from both quotidian reality and from a dreamscape full of "mirages without evaporation." A born naturalist, Nakazawa folds mallard, ironwood, yarrow, coulee, wetland and moonflower into her lines, creating an "origami dream" of flora and fauna. In one of this book's celebratory poems ("Sojourn to the Countryside"), we encounter those seeds "wanting to believe in a better world / seeds for short enduring joys, and long encouraged prayers." Such seeds carry the kind of intent evident throughout Nakazawa's work.

—Paulann Petersen, Oregon Poet Laureate Emerita

Pulse and Weave

LIZ NAKAZAWA

Flowstone Press

Pulse and Weave

Text and Cover Image Copyright © 2022 Liz Nakazawa

First Flowstone Press Edition • October 2022
ISBN 978-1-945824-60-9

Flowstone Press,
an Imprint of Left Fork
www.leftforkbooks.com

To the tree that gave up its life
to be pages in a book

and to Kay Frank

TABLE OF CONTENTS

I.

Empty	5
Clouds Unfold Into a Dream	6
Fate of Rain	7
Aspiration	8
The Missoula Flood	9
On My Walk	12
Nothing	13
Afternoon in the Public Garden	14
Nature's Oeuvre	15
Tone Painting	16
Olneya tesota	17

II.

Bones	21
Searching for My Hands in a Dream	22
Asleep	23
Reading Tea Leaves	24
Before I Die	25
Dream Group	26
Golden	27
Maundy Thursday: Five Loaves, Two Fishes	28

III.

Pendulous	33
Autumn	34
Japanese Garden in the Rain	35
A Portal into Spring	36
The Way of Tea	37
Thirty Miles From Womb Canyon	38
Four Rooms in Your Heart	39
Daughter of a Nez Perce Mom	40
Pray As Earth Does	41

IV.

Visit	45
Giving You	46
Arabesque	47
Helen Keller	48
Beginning Drawing for Seniors	49
From Tibet	51
Surrender	52
The Day Before the Night	54
For My Son	55
Three Haiku	56
Ocean Chant	57
Letter to You, Jellyfish	58
Tor House of Robinson Jeffers	59
Sojourn to the Countryside	61
A Blind Date With Nature	62
Helix	63

Acknowledgments	65

Pulse and Weave

I.

EMPTY

On the birdless day at the refuge
the morning was lento
cattails barely moving in breeze.

The canal twisted
dreaming
its dream paired with cumulous clouds above
trees knocking in wind: their colloquial speech
noon in parentheses
landscape absent of narrative drive.

No songs.

Just the day before I'd mentioned to a friend
minimal differences: beak size
feather pattern
stance on branch
white eye-ring circling eye.

But birds molt in secret come summer
begin looking messy, away from inquisitive eyes and field guides
missing and growing feathers create gaps in wing
sometime even a missing tail
pre-basic molt, summer plumage
each feather formed in a horny sheath.

With no birds
innocence dried and stilled
like a fermata of Shubert's held extra long.

Absent common tern, cliff swallow and sparrow
only bush shadows nod and azure sky.

CLOUDS UNFOLD INTO A DREAM

You could say all dreams are lies
but I insist I sent that
letter: both my first and my last
purple letter without stamp, signature or ink.

You could say I signed both letter and dream
the signature had already folded and disappeared
into a cloud and the cloud
unfolding into a dream

a dream, fragrant in folded paper
an original, blue origami dream
almost uncovered by dreamer
the dreamer disappearing into day.

FATE OF RAIN

It's Imbolc, February second, and we're
at the refuge. You point out
differences between ducks, coots and mallards
and when I ask you if you believe in prayer
you don't say a thing.

Like the Gaels, I silently
welcome a bit more of light's return.
But the Pagans did more
on this cross-quarter day of smithcraft and healing:
if it was foul weather the Cailleach hag
gathered firewood and tried spotting serpents
emerging from winter dens.
If clear, she slept in to declare an early spring.

You pull me back to cattails and nutria.
We spy a golden eagle
land and devour prey:
a flash of red, an open belly,
and the bird oblivious to time of year.

ASPIRATION

Like adding to a *penjing*,
the tiny landscape of pebbles and miniature tree,
you pick up, from below the dawn redwood, its cone,
an ounce of terrarium,
a split world rupturing into seas,
and place it in your pocket.

You imagine oceanic gases
mimicking the artificial breath of your friend
that canister that was draped in his lap the day before,
his wheelchair-bound wounds
of spirits and smoke exposed.

You had traveled to China together,
where this redwood, *metasequoia,* was born,
(I give you this tree's name now as offering)
needles shed in the cold of winter,
bark exfoliating and fissured,
with a hint of marquetry
reaching for firmament,
a living fossil 50 million-years-old.

You don't feel terror in the limitations of his
marrow, and explain to me that
all his journeys and piquant language
won't wither but will mix
and ferment with tundra and ice,
yarrow and tiger, grape skin,
nebula, peony and cloud.

THE MISSOULA FLOOD

I.

Deep in the Bitterroot Mountains
a finger from the Cordilleran ice sheet
moved south, through
the Purcell Trench
damned the Clark Fork River:
gave birth to Glacial Lake, Missoula.

Behind this plug
water rose and swelled
filling the valleys
to the east, the glacier buoyant,
and what wanted to be a river escaped
beneath the ice dam

draining the lake
and sending whorls of water to grind rocks
a race
through the Clark and Flathead Rivers,

picked apart bedrock
stripped topsoil
chiseled mazes
of buttes and canyons

Palouse soils scoured deep,
prow-shaped sculpturing
of gravel bars,
water-torn coulees and plug-pool basins.

In the Upper Coulee the churning river
yanked chunks of rock
from the face of the falls,
flooding collected in the Pasco Basin
pooled at Wallula Gap and then burst into the Columbia.

II.

Disaster, someone once said,
is something wrong with the stars.

Was all this
a natural tumult, or a furious
rampage of our insecure earth,
a flood with very little reverence
and no misgivings,
impudent rogue waves lumbering
west to the Pacific?

Three days later it was all over
and the beast was sung to sleep.

III.

The air was hollow and quiet
and the silence, fecund,
presaging the generosities
of fifteen-thousand years later,
the flood's begetting:
the fertile valley's mint,
a vineyard snaking up a gorged cliff,
grapes of the loam's prime terroir,
and the swale of spring.

ON MY WALK

On my walk
I gave up all ideas of evolution and atomic theory
regaling, instead, in sublime sauntering
bewildered strawberries to my left
cabbage in deep thought to my right
all this didgeridoo trumpeting of summer.

And who has not walked
in worthy moments
wandering
in unpredictable lengths of weather

becoming one of the fellows who goes it alone
a legato of striding
garrulous
excited
heedless
a little bit mad
semi-mechanical

an allegory of emptiness
stitched to landscape, wind and sky?

NOTHING

Birds, like people,
prefer boundaries: white throated sparrow
and magnolia warblers, symbiont and hugging hedgerows
roost sites with supply of berries
crabapple, hornbeam and holly.

On the far side of our boundaries
threads the old nothingness
where the permanent wrestles with quicksand
and times when the crop rotation of our hearts
appear then disappear
when thought blurs to Prussian blue, crimson lake and gamboge.

The riparian, the wetlands embracing river and stream,
cradles the birds within their aviary, keening for their dead
whole flocks circle back to where their fellow bird has fallen.

Come, speak to me of the empty
and the zone where we're most confused
and how benevolent negation
strengthens what remains.

AFTERNOON IN THE PUBLIC GARDEN

We come here to name flowers
one hundred, half the number
of bones in the body
count your spine, too.

A labyrinthine hedge
now contains us.
On the weathered bench you begin:
the myth of the Minotaur

part man, part bull
son of Pasiphaë
a creature imprisoned in the labyrinth
where he was fed maidens and men.

As you speak
all around us are interpreters
sparrows in their own way, bees
even clovers have tongues.

Cryptomeria lingers down a stone wall,
like peacock feathers you say
and then simile and metaphor stop
just at bold cliff over river barely in view

where Indians chased elk
and they became food,
no containment, just a strange
splashing cry.

NATURE'S OEUVRE

tableau of Gerry oak
giving me permission
to say hello to birch: my imaginary friend

birds suggesting
an ambiguity of skies
shadow of sleep
in a canon of fences
goatherds sleep

behind a mask of ivy
hunt of rich hummus

divagation of daffodils
ambient azaleas
repetitions of quivering aspen
boasting their trunks' theme

excommunicating winter
spring, though exhaustive flowerings
spring
doing its own thing

TONE PAINTING

How does this season get away
with it: all the frenzied repetitions
of daffodils and daisies
madrigal of lilies
endless bards of heather
canons of buttercups
and the call and response of crickets
between Old Testament trees?

Oh, hear ye of March's pitch and satisfactions
harmonies of sun and soil
wooing boundless metaphors
of white camellia
sheltering anaphora of pink tulips
sublimity of hyacinth and
nightingale, coo-coo and quail.

In this splendor, life
and death break bread
and an upmost wisteria rages on vine.
Hellebores nip and tuck.

The neighbor child's chalk drawing
dormant on sidewalk before rain
pink rose petals sprinkled (in her self-portrait) for hair.

OLNEYA TESOTA

giving it my full attention
to say its name aloud: ironwood
speaking of the leaves more slowly than how it's silently read

within the tale of ironwood someone was asked to find
their Achilles heel
that thing which has the power to destroy
if not addressed

but leaving mythology alone I pull
out my sample
to make sure this is the tree that's on my mind

the tree I nabbed leaves from pulls in and around base
creating shelter for bats and turtles
seeking safety from other animals and the sun

bark broke open
six to nine leaves on petiole

one of its leaves in my hand
now tracing the heart line in my palm
Olneya tesota, the Latin sings,

Olneya tesota

II.

BONES

The inherited farm
deep in our tissues,
throb like the small tortoise butterfly
entering the skinny kid's soul.

That long view of time,
embedded in the Eurasian collared-dove's song,
simply makes sense
in our bodies.

And the one man who studies red knot shorebirds
his entire life: how they travel
through the landscape to see
but not be seen.

Just like us:
instead of entering a city square
diagonally
we move, bones of caution,
around its edge.

SEARCHING FOR MY HANDS IN A DREAM

floating like a dream
knuckles lie fallow
bones hidden
beneath a lit up life line
heart line read quietly by the night
darkness and bloodline accepting
the finality of
morning murmuring of
fate line left empty.

ASLEEP

In the dream there are windows without light
In the dream there's air but no breathing
In the dream birds fly without song
In the dream there is nostalgia but no regrets
In the dream the house of cards never collapses
In the dream a few lines become a picture
In the dream there's vision but no knowledge
In the dream there is hysteria but no lungs

In the dream, costumes and scenery are on stage without actors
In the dream mailboxes contain mailed letters but no envelopes
In the dream there are gestures but no hands
In the dream there is an alibi without an original name
In the dream a labyrinth appears with no paths
In the dream there are mirages without evaporation

The dream displays a portrait of what someone will become
  but no being

READING TEA LEAVES

*Put a pinch of tea leaves in a blue cup
pour boiling water over them, steeping three minutes*

The person whose fortune is to be told is the "sitter" who takes cup by handle in the left hand rim upwards to the sky, moving it in rapid circles from left to right

Some tea leaves cling to the sides
others remain at the bottom

and then the reading begins
revealing careful, unseen moments
rigor, chagrin or regret

time below tender clouds
mistakes in false or true days
of nautical twilight

the March page forgotten to
be torn off the calendar
of desires of calm and repose

BEFORE I DIE

Before I die
I'll give you
a gesture of blessing
sudden bird
a story that can't be true
the shyness of violets
praise of jasmine scent.

I'll show you
the divinity of almonds
peek-a-boo of sunrise
the homecoming of hands
and saintliness of lemons.

Before I die
bring me a box
of your troubles
and I'll offer you
a velvet-wrapped ribboned balm.

DREAM GROUP

Holding up your catcher's mitt
to the bird flying straight at you
the next frame of the dream
reveals bird in the glove
with only one side showing: the left
eye filling with blood.

In the circle we all become the bird,
the wind, and the trees, the life list
and become those who identified the bird the week before.

An artist might fill in details:
blue plumage
black wing bar
nape
and white crown

bird both harbinger and omen
no noise, just that mitt poised.

Most birds have hollow bones, no marrow,
so they can more easily fly
but this bird's bones were filled with dream images
and that terrible dead song.

GOLDEN

no suddenness in the sanctum
just your holiness full of thanks, jasmine and blessing
moss and fern give you outline
the sun places its light on your shoulders
allowing descending rays of grace to appear
quiet as water peppermint and orchis
sacred, yellow and happy

we turn next to the autumn clock,
                                  to the sharing hour

MAUNDY THURSDAY:
FIVE LOAVES, TWO FISHES

Three Lavelle hawthorns outside
this door, lead me to the chapel.
I come because I need goblets, lilies and candles.
The organ begins the call.
In the notes are everyone
I've ever loved
and companions to silence, this song.
Pioneers from the East
formed this church with effort and prayer.

We hear words about kindling light
blessings and the breaking of bread across knees,
lambs across shoulders
salt, fresh water, honey-sweetened milk
and that from our blindness we can grow.

III.

PENDULOUS

the complicated anatomy of figs
punctuation of acorns
and deeply moral
grapes, urging their own completion
of purple, reflect upon
what is substantial in autumn

nothing in this season
moves too far away from sun
and the silliness of summer
reverts to careful

hours of days
shortening
toward upcoming icicles and frozen seed
relentless spiders interpret their craft
of innocence in amber light
and tall, definite grasses
hide poetry in their sheen

AUTUMN

The leaves and petioles anamnesis
forms what washed autumn calls its thesis
a cathedral of scarlet, yellow and red
petticoats covering branches' soft beds.

Branches patulous against a southern sky
read by squirrels' quick cry
petioles errant, throbbing and shy
we'll have neither spring nor summer instead.

O, give me autumn's pulsating door
open to this season's glorious shores.

JAPANESE GARDEN IN THE RAIN

Peeking through the pink azaleas
on the other side of bamboo
framed by maple:
seven mossy stones erupt
from circles of wet, white gravel.

Seven stones, including a mama stone,
seven, the same number
of lotus leaves
Buddha stepped out on when he was born.

Gardeners here cut leaves
of the bamboo
expose notched trunk
and prune bushes by hand.

I imagine instead of fog
a sunny day
and then decide
no, I promise to love this brash rain.

Cold lantern stares
at the cleft of Korean dogwood
reflected in the pond
a koi swims through branches.

A PORTAL INTO SPRING

O, spring morning's graceful gratitude, a musical prayer,
green with purple and pink generosities on heliotropic stems
winter bore you (that proud, shriveled *mise en scene*)
this day's daring beauty, all part of a theme.

Sing me, simple, ambassador of this brightening day
urge me to grow more bountiful and bountifully play
or sing of you myriad, tender, not staid
reenchant me, too, while on your loveliest I lean.

THE WAY OF TEA

The woman is shy but the tea is bold
she kneels at ninety degrees to the guest
pulls out unglazed stoneware
of coiled bands of clay
show of slow cleanliness
of bamboo tea scoop.

Ah, the gate to tea is wide
a triangle of red napkin
tucked into obi of indigo and white kimono
(the kimono of five-thousand years)
and with a lift of lid,
the ladle quiets the room,
outside:
spring rain,
         one weeping Yoshino cherry tree.

THIRTY MILES FROM WOMB CANYON

Here is the place where rabbits
gather: Puye, a land
of bone awl and perfect stones
fitting to potters' hands.

You look through a telescope
at a petroglyph, part turtle,
half bird, the jagged line of cliff
slicing our shared sky.

A thousand years ago
an upper floor fell, collapsing a jar
clay pieces shattered into
different rooms below.

I imagine men in breechcloth capes and leggings
and women of buckskin shawl
pounding yucca woven into cordage of rope
and sandal, painting pots with ground galena.

In the Tewe language
of this pueblo, a nearby village was
named Valley of Wild Rose but today
no scents in juniper wind.

FOUR ROOMS IN YOUR HEART

don't keep only one open
pray to all of them

some corners could frighten
but there're also sculptures of ease

praise window and door
and the intimacy of enclosed spaces

bearing meridians
and the forgiveness of the rooms' divisions

equally laugh and cry
awake to the outside of seed and soil

DAUGHTER OF A NEZ PERCE MOM

Past the campground and before the old threshing barn
a sign points left to Kitty Newell's Grave.
I arrived the empty way
to be alone and lonely
facing the granite stone
matching its solitude
in a madrigal of wildflower and wood.

Ten paces from any stream for reflection
I wondered: were there ever statues
of the trapper father and Kitty
who married a Nez Perce here?

And why does she lie east of Champoog Creek
when west of the water was her home?
Sky opened in answer to this land,
one of the few places western bluebirds still nest
white bars on their wings.

PRAY AS EARTH DOES

hold others steady
be a cradle for seed
absorb water slowly
help feed the hungry
manifest layer of rock
so young children
delight in its pebbles
hold others steady
crumble when needed
let others burrow in you
sharing their sorrows
hold others steady
be a friend to moles and badgers
hold others steady
be a lap for horse chestnut, catalpa and fir
hold others steady
warm with the sun
pray: to hold others steady

IV.

VISIT

after you arrive I will have forgotten about
the decorative hiatus when time was
a planet moving retrograde

will have forgotten all the accidental notes
and vagaries of nature: ladybug spots
in a myriad of number, throbbing dew in petal
but will still remember my log jammed heart

and when you arrive you'll feel my pulse
all the way to Greenland

GIVING YOU

clean sheets
and slow-cooked soups
moonflowers
aprons full of plum blossoms
flutter of a heart's wing
the comfort of a song lyric's rhymes
dalliance of light scattered on a sundial
and the shape of the sea

ARABESQUE

on the wings of your confusion
(or my own)
are lit sweet candles
that help scent our way

feet
on jade stepping stones
of couples that came before
our coupling

we share water
wonder
wading
in shallows
between mure and murmurings
our river both flooding and docile

I run to the dictionary
and beckon towards the pages
realizing it served us our wine
the vine of lush vocabulary
we used to feverishly
fall into
shared hourglass

someday we'll hop on
a shallop painted
white and blue
you: rowing
me: enveloped in the *dal segno*
of our song

HELEN KELLER

When word opened to world
Anne spelling
doll
water
key
into Helen's hand
after she'd opened her palm
thirsty palm to Anne's midwifery of lullaby and psalm
Helen's hands: just the right tilt and distance from the sun

behind no veil or scrim
only word hymn
the pasturage of nouns pointing here
                here.

That was when word grew to world
behind Helen's eyelids
bereft of dark or light
just blossom,
                blossom.

BEGINNING DRAWING FOR SENIORS

In this square room
there is nothing of our demise
no choking, slipping, falling
no frenzied beeping monitors or exposure of vein
just rapt objects
on the table in the center of our circle:
cube
triangle
square
rectangle
watering can
cylinder
and their accompanied demands:
the struggle of white paper and charcoal.

Eye-hand coordination,
drawing, like driving
or diving into a particular spot in the pool,
gets tricky.

Pascal helps us ask
in how many ways is it possible to arrange a group of objects
(square
watering can
rectangle
cylinder
triangle
cube)
or the lines in a poem?

Outside our windows the day pretends not to see
all of us insecure in drawing class.
Ginkgo leaves, aping tiny
Japanese fans tango in the breeze.
Clothespins harness bedding to a thin line.
Two people walking,
one points out her companion's contradictions.

The season, paused before turning,
waits for the eyes' irises to catch up.

Drawing now with charcoal
we are yoked to our bodies:
our sometimes unforgiving companions,
bodies with eyes and hands
being taught
to draw,

drawing six objects that speak
for us to listen.

FROM TIBET

From your wheelchair
you say you came to this country for freedom
after the Chinese bombed
the monasteries and monks of your dreams.
You offer me *momo*
your t-shirt boasting a yak: the animal
whose beads of bone are sold in China.
After some pleated moments between us
you wheel into your space of color
your prayer room circled by matchbook-sized
flags of blue and yellow.

Putting myself to bed later with
the smell of your gift of sandalwood incense,
woodsy with hints of vanilla,
I think of that tangled immigration
from your country of sky burial
where corpses were once wrapped in
white cloth and placed in homes' corners
for three days, then offered to mountains,
up to devouring vultures.

Yaks do best above 10,000 feet.
I pray in smoke that in our country
you'll have enough air.

SURRENDER

Dear Mom,
Wind chimes clatter
made from hollow bones
of your own parents',
sprouting your dissociation.

I was fire and red, you, blue and frozen
murmurations through your tourniquet
of *via negativa* parenting.

In silent films
there were occasional cues
orienting the viewer, such as "Twenty Years Later"
or "Back at Home."

But you fed me no east, no west,
no north or south.
The compass that never appeared
rusts now, Mother, and rests,
and your letters (the only threshold to any of your love)
crumble yellow, while
needs fold, stay content in tinged drawers.

Some day I could compose
cello music for you
but wolf tones might appear
so let's leave it there, Mom,
dear Holograph Mom.

A year after your passing
(your ashes buried in my backyard hosta)
I offer myself
a comfy legal term:
compassionate release.

No longer busking for love,
I can sing now in quiet
decent octaves of my own.

THE DAY BEFORE THE NIGHT

as light is captured
within the dark
you carried a candle on your dying lips
and miracles cocooned in the mundane
since this could be an ordinary act
my touch on your skin
the day before that holiness of night

like a familiar dream
dropped from the void
you slumbered
each breath taking longer to appear
then there were no archetypes
just your bones
stretched beyond sacrifice and obedience
and word retreating into shadow

the poetry of your brow,
blossoming toward some gentle
darkness at the back of the eye

FOR MY SON

you and I were up on the butte
our city lay below us
like a big skirt puffed with memory
when I spoke of the anchor we all need

not a real anchor, you knew,
though a few times it felt I could hold it in my hand
but the anchor full of good humor and generosity
which doesn't change when the world lurches and moves

it contains no color but holds the best of who we are
it doesn't breathe seasons but memory of seasons
anchor with none of the fervor of inborn ears
hearing headlines, neighborhood gossip or thoughts of giving up

big themes remain tragic
while our anchors fish the daily joys

THREE HAIKU

one brick missing
space
for a prayer

                                      sand in an hourglass
                                      pulling
                                      the last perennial

               in the cemetery
               a river
               unravels

OCEAN CHANT

not all angels have wings
perhaps many are simply ships with big sails

all of us: boat builders
with windlass to hoist anchor, rotation by turn of a crank

navigate me, help empty my hull
then fill me with your ennui or woe

let's dodge buoys together
search bottom of sea to fish mirth

cephalopoda laugh bilaterally
waving down there with tentacles

they are angels, too, with their own nets
waiting on sand beneath sea

LETTER TO YOU, JELLYFISH

Dear Jellyfish,
Thank you for dancing in the Salish Sea
the same waters shared by the Makah, Nootsak and Nisqually
dancing and swimming night as well as day
a little night music
the way you swim
symmetrical
though sometimes still
a pattern, but with irregular rhythm
jazz among minnows
one long baptism in the Salish Sea
a sea stretched from the Strait of Georgia
to the southern end of Puget Sound.

Some scientists say you taste like tofu
and all agree you have no brain
gelatinous, medusa, polyp
moon jelly, lion's mane jelly
Who are you? No matter
Swimming to charm me in the Salish Sea.

TOR HOUSE OF ROBINSON JEFFERS

At the cusp of land and sea in Carmel
we enter the dark cottage where
Robin and Una read Robert Louis Stevenson to the twins
(their small laundry flapping in the wind)
by candle, wrote and played chess,
the red horse and queen
now safely behind glass.

Rarely working in wood, only stone,
when he first began
building his home, one quiet stone following
stone, Santa Lucia granite, local rock,
rolled one at a time uphill from the beach
bereft of a team of horses.

Then there were the mad additions: a top
stone from a pyramid of Giza
salvaged slabs of a shipwreck's ballast
abalone from an Ohlone Indian
encampment on this land
obsidian from Mt. Shasta
slate from the Officer's Club at Fort Ord
Portuguese tile, a gravestone nabbed

from a church in Ireland
that the Jeffers carried across
the country in their model-T.
Una said the stone turned her blood
to water and reminded her
of home in County Down.
Robin wrote poetry in the morning and worked
on the house most afternoons while Una collected
wildflower seeds from everywhere and Irish ballads.

All the books he loved are veiled
behind thin, gold diamond-shaped netting.
I squint to see titles as our guide
points to the 1911 Britannica,
the only book on display.

We're shown how the couple loved to
write on the wall in the den,
some Spencer on a dark high beam
a line from "The Faerie Queene"
where the Red Cross Knight pursues the good.

In the bedroom we're led and are read
the poem about the death bed before us,
which Robin both hated and revered
and the one he died in during
that unusual California snow,
the same snow that fell the day he was born.

I wasn't sure what phase the moon was in during
our tour but thought perhaps the tide had
receded a bit since the time
Una sewed white shirts with collars
so her husband would look more
like a poet and one daily hawk watched
Jeffers hew with stone.

SOJOURN TO THE COUNTRYSIDE

I want to tell you about my drive today
hugging the river
how our fears evaporate on sunny days,
that this farmland cradles the oldest barn in Oregon
and there are seeds there wanting to believe in a better world
seeds for short, enduring joys, and long, encouraged prayers.

Hayden's quartet was on the radio
and he bid the violin to dream
while the sheep were asleep on a green knoll full of lyrical
    confessions.

Nothing in those farms of belief or certainty
just leaves, veggies, stone and tree, fifty miles from the sea.

A BLIND DATE WITH NATURE

Before meeting her I sewed bigger pockets on my dress
knowing stones might fill them
once the blindfold came off
and I'd be crushed by color, form and designs:

    The geometrics of pasture and cow
    geodes linking bare feet to soil
    amethyst, lavender anklet on skin
    the nipple of spring and fantasia of fall
    mushroom as still as a corpse
    trickster toadstools
    coloratura of seaweed
    amulet of anemone
    the scriptorium of blue-green coral reef beneath shoal
    millipedes with mojo
    a pokerfaced platypus
    birthery of buttercups
    the go-to of gossamer wings

and smultronställe: that remote place where wild strawberries grow.

After removing the blindfold
I became the texture of sea urchin's custard and cream
and a granddaughter to allostratus clouds

whistling while a moss melody and lilac lyric held hands.

HELIX

I wake with watermelon
in duet with last night's dream

check my well for water
watch light balance on the sundial
notice the downy woodpecker looking less confused.

I wake
and separate the knower from the known
brush dirt from a hidden turquoise tile
smile
inhale vials of fragrance
glance at the rainbow flicker in the prism of dew
languid in the petal of a rose.

I wake
do a frenzied dance to symbols everywhere
the ancient ones crouching in the belly of the day.

I wake
and calligraph the morning
stitch it to afternoon

the wheel of evening graces towards midnight,
then awakes to thank you for omega morning.

ACKNOWLEDGMENTS

Grateful acknowledgment to the following places where several poems were first published.

Lucky Jefferson (Spring 2020) — "Surrender"

Painting the Heart Open (2019) (chapbook) The Poetry Box — "Clouds Unfold Into a Dream"
"Golden"
"Tor House of Robinson Jeffers"
"Pendulous"
"Pray As Earth Does"

The Poeming Pigeon (2017) — "Tone Painting
"Giving You"

Remmington Review (Summer 2022) — "Sojourn to the Countryside"

Rock and Sling (Spring 2019) — "From Tibet"

Timberline Review (Summer/Fall 2015) — "The Missoula Flood"

Turn (2013) Uttered Chaos Press — "Fate of Rain"

Willawaw (Spring 2021) — "Empty"

ABOUT THE AUTHOR

Liz Nakazawa has edited two collections of poetry by Oregon poets: *Deer Drink the Moon: Poems of Oregon* and *The Knotted Bond: Oregon Poets Speak of Their Sisters*. *Deer Drink the Moon* was listed as one of "150 Books for 150 Years of Statehood," announced by the Oregon State Library and *Poetry Northwest* in 2009 (poetrynw.org/824) and was also a Best Pick of Powell's. Her own poems have appeared in *The Timberline Review*, *The Poeming Pigeon*, *Willawa*, *Turn*, *Amythyst Review*, *Rock and Sling*, *Remington Review* and *ahundredgourds*.

She writes essays, takes photos, enjoys walking, swimming and choreographing dances, and is a practitioner of calligraphy in addition to writing poetry. She feels grateful to be living in this bounteous and wondrous world.

www.ingramcontent.com/pod-product-compliance
Lightning Source LLC
Chambersburg PA
CBHW030350100526
44592CB00010B/899